S0-GQE-985

A Towel Filled with Toothpaste

Kimberly Henry

A Towel Filled With Toothpaste

Copyright © 2016 Kimberly Henry

All rights reserved.

ISBN:1540523748
ISBN-13:9781540523747

DEDICATION

I dedicate this book back to God. Thank you for showing me your forgiveness, faithfulness, and love.

A Towel Filled With Toothpaste

CONTENTS

A Towel Filled With Toothpaste

A Towel Filled With Toothpaste

INTRODUCTION

This devotional is comprised of posts from my personal Facebook page. They are in no particular chronological order. Each day contains a Facebook post, scripture, and a look into how God uses my children to point me to Him. My children often direct me to God through humor, but sometimes it's through frustration or even awe. I am convinced that God can be seen everywhere in everything if we will open our eyes to see Him.

My children are:
Addison Joy, Noah Benjamin, & Owen Alexander.

A Towel Filled With Toothpaste

DAY 1 – NEW CREATIONS

While waiting for Addison to arrive home on the school bus, we see a fuzzy yellow caterpillar with long black spikes crawling on our porch.

Noah: Eewww. Mommy, what is THAT?!?

Me: It's just a weird looking caterpillar. It'll
        probably turn into something really cool.

Noah: Like a CROCODILE?!?

LOL

That would be really cool, wouldn't it? Just imagine all kinds of interesting looking caterpillars turning into crocodiles!

This reminds me of our lives after we choose to follow Jesus. Before we knew Jesus, we were just a bunch of weird looking caterpillars. After we accept Him as our savior and follow Him, He transforms our lives into something totally different. The Bible says that when we come to Christ we become a new creation.

"So from now on we regard no one from a worldly point of view. Though we once regarded Christ in this way, we do so no longer. Therefore, if

1

anyone is in Christ, the new creation has come: The old has gone, the new is here! All this is from God, who reconciled us to himself through Christ and gave us the ministry of reconciliation: that God was reconciling the world to himself in Christ, not counting people's sins against them. And he has committed to us the message of reconciliation. We are therefore Christ's ambassadors, as though God were making his appeal through us. We implore you on Christ's behalf: Be reconciled to God. God made him who had no sin to be sin for us, so that in him we might become the righteousness of God." (2 Corinthians 5:16-21)

When we choose to follow Christ, God forgives us of all of our past sins. He takes our old, fuzzy, weird, spiky life and turns it into something beautiful for His glory. Does this happen instantly? Not usually. Caterpillars have to spend some time in a tight, dark cocoon before becoming butterflies. We may seem to be stuck in a cocoon of darkness, but don't let that discourage you. Anger, disappointment, selfishness, and worry can morph into love, contentment, generosity, and peace. We can eventually look like completely different creatures after being transformed by the love of God.

The Bible says that we are new creations, and that we are not to look at others with a "worldly point of view." When you look at others, try to see them for the creations that they can be in Christ. Share the message of His love and forgiveness.

God has done some amazing transformations in the past. He is constantly shaping me into something new. There is no telling what really cool creation you will become if you allow God to transform you. You could be a beautiful butterfly, a puppy, or maybe even a crocodile!

DAY 2 - TREASURE

Addison: Mom, I wish I had a metal detector to find treasure.

Me: Oh yeah?

Addison: Then I wouldn't have to keep wandering around looking for an 'x'!

LOL

Are you looking for an 'x'? Sometimes I can get caught-up in looking at the newest fashions or big fancy houses with all new appliances, but then I have to remind myself that I already have a lot of treasure. I have a husband who loves God, three children, and a home to live in. The Bible mentions treasure in the book of Matthew.

"Do not store up for yourselves treasures on earth, where moths and vermin destroy, and where thieves break in and steal. But store up for yourselves treasures in heaven, where moths and vermin do not destroy, and where thieves do not break in and steal. For where your treasure is, there your heart will be also." (Matthew 6:19-21)

3

If we continually search for an 'x', our lives can become empty. We can pour all of our time into our career trying to capture more and more wealth. We can dress ourselves in all the newest trendy clothes, drive fancy new cars, eat the finest foods, and take lavish vacations. These things by themselves are not bad, but if we are always consumed with having bigger and better things, our hearts will never be truly satisfied. All of these material things can be taken away in the blink of an eye. The Bible cites moths and vermin, but our modern-day treasures can also be taken by flood, fire, lawsuits, etc.

Our treasures don't always have to be material in nature. Placing all of our love and hope in our spouse or children will never completely fulfill us either. While it makes us feel good to love and serve them, they are only human and will eventually, at times, make us sad, frustrated, or angry. We cannot depend on them for our happiness and joy.

If we store up treasures in heaven, they can never be taken from us by things of this world. What can we do to store up treasures in heaven? Visit with a lonely widow. Prepare a meal for a sick friend. Donate things that you no longer use to people who are less fortunate. Take time to talk with a friend who needs a listening ear. We can all use our time more wisely to be kind to one another. Then we will store up true treasure.

DAY 3 - LISTEN & WAIT

A few minutes after having a deep conversation with Addison about our souls, praying, etc., I find her sitting on the countertop in our bathroom with her hand cupped to her ear. She was listening for Jesus and waiting for Him to talk to her.

How often do I take the time to sit in quiet and listen? Do I try to hear Jesus? Do I wait for even a few minutes for Him to speak to me?

"Don't you yet understand? Don't you know by now that the everlasting God, the Creator of the farthest parts of the earth, never grows faint or weary? No one can fathom the depths of his understanding. He gives power to the tired and worn out, and strength to the weak.. Even the youths shall be exhausted, and the young men will all give up. But they that wait upon the Lord shall renew their strength. They shall mount up with wings like eagles; they shall run and not be weary; they shall walk and not faint." (Isaiah 40:28-31 The Living Bible)

I usually pray when I wake up in the morning and just before I fall asleep at night. Too often I feel like my prayer time consists of thanking God for what He has given me and then immediately asking Him for a million other things. I ask for healing for specific individuals who are sick, a job for an unemployed friend, protection for missionary friends overseas – the list goes on and on. I don't think that God is too offended by this (I'm sure He hears requests 24 hours a day.), but does it really do much for our relationship? Relationships with mostly one-sided conversations can be tiring for both parties involved.

As a mom of three little kiddos, I'm almost always tired before I even begin to pray. By the time I am done with my lengthy list of requests I'm exhausted and usually fall asleep. The Bible says in Isaiah that God will give power to the tired and strength to the weak. There is a catch – we have to wait upon the Lord.

I think that God would enjoy us coming to Him with our hand cupped to our ear. We need to wait on Him and listen for His voice. We can still feel free to give Him praise and present our requests to Him, but if we take even a small amount of time to just wait for Him to speak to us, we will be blessed. It would be a real two-sided conversation. God can give us guidance, direction, and strength if we simply take the time to listen.

DAY 4 – PORK CHOP

I got a little reward for myself for losing some more baby weight. Kmart had jeans on sale, so I purchased a size smaller than normal and a few other items. After we left the store, I checked the receipt to make sure that the jeans were rung-up with the correct sale price. The price was correct, but the item description on the receipt read, "pork chop." LOL Apparently I have another size or two to lose!

I have since learned that "pork chop" refers to a particular style of pockets. This would explain why my jeans were recorded as such on my receipt, but I didn't have that knowledge at the time of purchase. I saw the words "pork chop" and felt simultaneous humor and defeat. Was I *ever* going to get my pre-baby body back? I had been working really hard to lose some weight. Did I still look like a pork chop?

While wallowing in disappointment with my pitiful self, God hit me with a hard truth - a truth that most people don't hear often enough. It is this: God is more concerned about the size of our heart than the size of our jeans.

We were not designed to look the same. God made each of us to look and act differently.

> *"For you created my inmost being; you knit me together in my mother's womb.*
>
> *I praise you because I am fearfully and wonderfully made; your works are wonderful, I know that full well.*
>
> *My frame was not hidden from you when I was made in the secret place, when I was woven together in the depths of the earth.*
>
> *Your eyes saw my unformed body; all the days ordained for me were written in your book before one of them came to be." (Psalm 139:13-16)*

Have you ever watched someone weave? It requires a design, precision, and time. God wove each of us together while we were in the womb. He took care in making us unique. I think that it's insulting to Him when we look into a mirror and tear-down what He created.

We can often feel judged by the world according to our appearance. We're too fat, too thin, too bald, too short, etc. The Bible says in 1 Samuel that people look at our outward appearance, but God looks at our heart.

We can honor God by taking care of the unique bodies that He's given us. We should strive to be happy and healthy, but we shouldn't stress about our weight or hair color. We please God when we concentrate more on loving Him and loving others rather than loving the number on the inside of our jeans.

DAY 5 – SMARTY PANTS

I was driving Addison to preschool today (after driving through many states while on vacation for the past 10 days) and she asks me, "Where are we at?"

I said, "We're in Pennsylvania. That's the name of our state."

She then says, "Actually Mommy, it's a commonwealth."

LOL I do remember teaching her that fact a few months ago, but I didn't think that she would actually remember!

Wow! What a wake-up call for this mama! My daughter was paying close attention to what I taught her. At the tender age of 4, she was listening to me. She was retaining all kinds of information. The Bible says in Proverbs 22:6, *"Train up a child in the way he should go: and when he is old, he will not depart from it."*

As a mom, I have the awesome privilege of training my children every day. I teach them about shapes, colors, letters, numbers, and nature. I also instruct my children in less glamorous areas such as toilet training and why it's important to eat their vegetables. While all of these things are exciting to learn, they pale in comparison to training my children about what's really important – how to follow God.

My daughter's smarty pants response to my reply made me realize that she is paying very close attention to me and she remembers my words. She will also remember my actions. I need to remember that my children are always watching me. What am I training them to do?

I should be training my children to follow God. God gave us Jesus as the perfect teacher. I need to follow His words and His examples. Jesus was kind. He showed compassion. He took time to pray. Do I do those things in front of my children?

I am responsible for the training of my children. Sunday School teachers are wonderful, but they only instruct our children for an hour or two each week. I can't possibly expect my kids to learn everything that they need to know about God and the Bible from two hours with a Sunday School teacher. It's up to me to teach them about the ways of God. It's not enough to just explain these concepts. I need to model generosity, kindness, justice, mercy, and grace.

Whether we realize it or not, children are always watching us. They will repeat our words and actions. Are your words and actions something that you would be proud to have kids repeat?

DAY 6 – COUNTING SHEEP

Pony Grandma, Aunt Stephi, and Aunt Kelli would be proud of Addy. (My mother and sisters own horses.) She just came to me and told me that she couldn't sleep, so I explained to her about "counting sheep." She thought about the new concept for a few seconds and said, "That sounds good, but can I count horses instead?"

Do you ever have a difficult time falling asleep? Some nights it seems like I will never sleep. My brain refuses to be quiet. All of the events from the day replay through my mind. Then everything on my to-do list for the next day pops into my brain –

"Is Noah supposed to take snack for his class tomorrow?, I can't forget to mail the electric bill., Remember to pick Addy up at school for her doctor's appointment. I have to finish a project for work. What am I forgetting?"

I stress over how I am going to organize myself to make sure everything gets accomplished. I make lists and mark my calendar, but my brain still won't stop.

Sometimes the thoughts running through our brains aren't simply, "Who's lunch needs to be packed in the morning?" Sometimes our thoughts are consumed with much stronger burdens –

> "Will I be able to pay the mortgage?, How can I help my friend who has cancer?, Where can I get help for my aging parent?"

The list can go on and on. Counting sheep rarely works for these burdens, but there is someone who can help.

> *"Come to me, all you who are weary and burdened, and I will give you rest. Take my yoke upon you and learn from me, for I am gentle and humble in heart, and you will find rest for your souls. For my yoke is easy and my burden is light."*
> (Matthew 11:28-30)

Jesus tells us to come to Him. When we give Him our worries and burdens, He promises to give us rest. Jesus offers to trade yokes with us when we spend time with Him and learn from Him.

The next time you find yourself awake and weary, and counting sheep(or horses)doesn't help, try spending time with Jesus. He promises rest for your soul.

DAY 7 – BIG , STRONG DADDY

While helping Addison clean up her room we had the following conversation:

> Me: We'll put these totes full of clothes and shoes out here. We'll ask Daddy to carry them down to the basement and stack them.
>
> Addison: Because he's big and strong?
>
> Me: Yep.
>
> Addison: Just like God?
>
> Me: Something like that.

Little children often think of their fathers as the biggest, strongest people that they know. They believe that their daddys are invincible. I remember watching my father build our house. I remember riding on top of his shoulders through shopping malls. I remember him pushing towering wheel barrow loads of wood into our basement so that we could fill our stove and stay warm. My dad could also build or fix almost anything. (He still can.)

Do we think of our Heavenly Father in the same way? We need to remember that even though most of our earthly fathers are strong, they are weak compared to our Father in Heaven. He is bigger, stronger, and more powerful than we can even imagine. He created the whole world and everything in it, and He calls us His children. When was the last time that you were awed by God? Do you run to Him when you need help or protection?

Maybe you don't have a good relationship with your earthly father. If that's the case, take comfort in the fact that your Heavenly Father loves you and watches over you.

"I lift up my eyes to the mountains—
where does my help come from?
My help comes from the Lord,
the Maker of heaven and earth.
He will not let your foot slip—
he who watches over you will not slumber;
indeed, he who watches over Israel
will neither slumber nor sleep.
The Lord watches over you—
the Lord is your shade at your right hand;
the sun will not harm you by day,
nor the moon by night.
The Lord will keep you from all harm—
he will watch over your life;
the Lord will watch over your coming and going
both now and forevermore." (Psalms 121)

This psalm is my favorite. Whenever I am facing a struggle, I immediately go to this chapter. It reassures me that no matter what I am going through, my help comes from the Lord. If He is helping me, there is nothing that I can't overcome.

DAY 8 – POISONED

Addison just told Noah that their favorite kind of potato chips were "poisoned" and that he shouldn't eat any more. She whispered to me, "Put them back in the cabinet so I can eat the rest of them later." LOL I made her go back and share the chips with Noah. I think she can go from sweetheart to stinker in about three seconds.

Our sinful, selfish nature – it rears its ugly head even in a five-year-old child. Chips aren't the only snack that she hoards. This is the same child who hides individual sundae cones in various places in the freezer so that her father can't find them.

To be honest, I can be selfish too. Who hasn't tucked away the last Little Debbie snack cake behind the vegetables in the refrigerator? I can't be the only one. The Bible gives us direction when it comes to the topic of selfishness.

> "Do nothing out of selfish ambition or vain conceit. Rather, in humility value others above yourselves, not looking to your own interests but each of you to the interests of the others.
> In your relationships with one another, have the same mindset as Christ Jesus:

Who, being in very nature God,
    did not consider equality with God something to
be used to his own advantage;
  rather, he made himself nothing
    by taking the very nature of a servant,
    being made in human likeness.
And being found in appearance as a man,
  he humbled himself
    by becoming obedient to death—
      even death on a cross!" (Philippians 2:3-8)

I don't think that the apostle Paul is referring to hiding treats in this passage, but the message is clear. We shouldn't be selfish. We are to follow Jesus' example. He was humble and put us above Himself. He died for me and you.

We're supposed to look out for others before ourselves. That's not the message that the world around us teaches. We're bombarded from everywhere with messages like, "Look out for number one" or "Do what makes you happy."

While it's good to take care of ourselves, we have to be aware of the needs of others if we want to be more like Christ. We can donate money to charity, help a coworker when they are struggling with a project, or volunteer at a nursing home. If examples like this sound difficult, maybe you can start with something small, like sharing your favorite potato chips. Don't let the "poison" of selfishness hold you back from showing the love of God.

DAY 9 – ANNIVERSARY

Addison: Mommy, what's that?
Me: It's an anniversary card. I've been married to Daddy for eight years now.
Addison: WOW! I'm so proud of you!
LOL

My husband and I have now been married for over thirteen years. Some days I am pretty proud of myself. Other days I'm pretty proud of my husband. Marriage isn't easy – even my three-year-old could see that fact. Two imperfect people are joined together with different backgrounds, personalities, and quirks. How do we make our relationships healthy and lasting?

"Love is patient, love is kind. It does not envy, it does not boast, it is not proud. It does not dishonor others, it is not self-seeking, it is not easily angered, it keeps no record of wrongs. Love does not delight in evil but rejoices with the truth. It always protects, always trusts, always hopes, always perseveres. Love never fails." (1 Corinthians 13:4-8a)

17

This passage of scripture is read at almost every wedding. It gives us God's definition of love. It's the formula for us to follow in order to have strong marriages that last a lifetime.

Even though my daughter is proud of me for staying married and loving her daddy, I know that it's not something that I accomplish in my own strength. It's God's love being displayed through me. The Bible says in 1 John 4, verse 19 that "We love because He first loved us." When we follow Jesus as our savior, His love is shown through us.

God loved us so much that he sent his son, Jesus, into the world to be our sacrifice and our example. God is patient, God is kind. I thank God that He doesn't keep a record of our wrongs. Loving someone is more than just acting according to our mushy feelings – it's a commitment. We won't always feel like loving everyone, but it's Jesus's strength in us that helps us to persevere.

While 1Corinthians 13 is usually read at weddings, it's not exclusive to married couples. God's definition of love works for all relationships. Trust and kindness go a long way with strengthening friendships and relationships with family members too.

If you're in a relationship now that's struggling, try practicing God's definition of love. Remember, God's love never fails.

DAY 10 – A NEW SONG

Addison wrote a new song for her daddy tonight. It goes a little something like this… "rooOOOAAST BEEEeeef, rooOOOOOOOOAAAAAASSSST BEEEEeeeeeef!" LOL

In case you haven't guessed, my husband really enjoys eating roast beef. He likes meat of all kinds, but red meat is his favorite. Addison wanted to show her daddy how much she loved him, so she decided to write a song that he would really like. She chose to sing about meat.

Initially, we were all laughing and having a good time with her new song, but then God spoke to my heart. After hearing Addison's song, it was like God was saying to me, "Listen to that. She loves her daddy so much that she wrote a song just for him. I love when my children write songs just for me!"

"Sing to the Lord a new song;
sing to the Lord, all the earth.
Sing to the Lord, praise his name;
proclaim his salvation day after day.
Declare his glory among the nations,
his marvelous deeds among all peoples.
For great is the Lord and most worthy of praise;
he is to be feared above all gods.

19

*For all the gods of the nations are idols,
but the Lord made the heavens.
Splendor and majesty are before him;
strength and glory are in his sanctuary.
Ascribe to the Lord, all you families of nations,
ascribe to the Lord glory and strength.
Ascribe to the Lord the glory due his name;
bring an offering and come into his courts.
Worship the Lord in the splendor of his
holiness; tremble before him, all the earth.
Say among the nations, 'The Lord reigns.'
The world is firmly established, it cannot be
moved; he will judge the peoples with equity.
Let the heavens rejoice, let the earth be glad;
let the sea resound, and all that is in it.
Let the fields be jubilant, and everything in
them; let all the trees of the forest sing for joy.
Let all creation rejoice before the Lord, for he
comes, he comes to judge the earth.
He will judge the world in righteousness
and the peoples in his faithfulness."(Psalm 96)*

The psalmist is very clear that we are to sing to the Lord. In fact, singing a new song is mentioned about five times in the book of Psalms. We are to sing, play musical instruments, and dance to show the greatness of our God.

Did you know that God sings too? In the book of Zephaniah, it's said that God will rejoice over the Israelites with singing.

When was the last time you sang to God? Take time today to sing a new song to God. Tell Him how great He is and how much you love Him.

DAY 11 – A TOWEL FILLED WITH TOOTHPASTE

How interesting it is to get out of a nice, warm shower and dry off with …a towel filled with toothpaste.

There I was, a busy mom who had stolen away some time to get a shower. I had put some cartoons on the television to entertain my kiddos for a few minutes. Apparently the show was not as enthralling as I had hoped. One or both of the children managed to enter the bathroom and open a tube of toothpaste. After squeezing some out of the tube, they decided to clean-up their mess with my bath towel. I finished my nice, warm shower and reached out through the curtain to grab my towel. After drying my legs for a few seconds, I realized that something wasn't right. I felt inside my towel. I smelled the inside of my towel. It was filled with toothpaste.

At that moment, I wanted to be upset. My warm, peaceful, relaxing shower had taken a turn for the worse. My leg and hands were now covered with toothpaste. It was then that God spoke to me. "Remember, your children are a blessing."

> *"Children are a heritage from the Lord,*
>   *offspring a reward from him.*
> *Like arrows in the hands of a warrior*
>   *are children born in one's youth.*
> *Blessed is the man whose quiver is full of*
>   *them." (Psalm 127:3-5a)*

Hahaha. Yes, they are. They are cute little blessings that cry, smash crackers on the floor, color on the walls, and fill towels with toothpaste. They are also little blessings that make silly faces, sing songs, help with chores, give great hugs, and say, "I love you, Mommy."

I decided to check my attitude. If getting smeared with toothpaste was the worst thing that happened to me that day, I was still truly blessed. My children were not my only blessings. I had a nice, safe house with electricity and indoor plumbing. I had food to eat. I had clothes to wear. I had a husband who loved me very much. I'm so thankful for that towel filled with toothpaste that helped me to keep things in perspective.

DAY 12 – ANGER

I was getting frustrated trying to help Noah get his pull-up on after using the potty. He kept kicking his legs and being goofy, so I eventually yelled, "STOP!" Without missing a beat Noah yelled back, "HAMMER TIME!" LOL

How could I possibly be angry with him after that response? Leave it to my silly middle child to save me from my anger. It was an ordinary, daily occurrence to help him with toilet training, but on this particular day I was tired and worn-out. I was trying desperately to get my children tucked into their beds so that I could get to my own bed that was calling my name. I didn't want to be goofy. I didn't want to dance around. I wanted to get his pull-up and jammies on him as fast as possible. Frustration was setting-in and anger was approaching.

I thank God for keeping me from becoming angry and saying or doing something foolish that I may regret. I'm reminded of the following passage in Ecclesiastes:

"Do not be quickly provoked in your spirit,
for anger resides in the lap of fools."
(Ecclesiastes 7:9)

I was letting my spirit become provoked. I was dangerously close to scolding my son and saying something that might crush his little dancing spirit. Instead, God brought humor into my situation. He used my son to squash my frustration. He took my anger and replaced it with joy.

I'm thankful that I serve a God so big and ingenious that He can use anything to teach me a lesson. Even the lyrics of M.C. Hammer.

DAY 13 – KETCHUP

Me: What do you and Noah want for lunch today?
Addison: Ketchup!
LOL...They split a grilled cheese sandwich, a banana, chips, and a brownie.

I know my daughter. I know that she absolutely loves ketchup. In fact, if I put a blob of ketchup on her plate with her food, she will save it till last and just eat it by itself so that she can savor the flavor. She even licks it off of her plate. Ketchup isn't bad, but I don't think that it qualifies as a healthy lunch all on its own. I gave my kids a lunch that I thought was more appropriate and beneficial. I didn't deny Addison a plate full of ketchup because I wanted to be mean and deny her request. I gave her something else because I love her and want what is best for her.

I wonder how many times God does the same thing for us. We ask Him for a specific automobile, promotion at work, deliverance from a health problem, etc. We pray feverishly asking for God to work in our lives so that we get these things, and sometimes He gives them to us. Other times God denies our requests.

As a young Christian, when God answered my prayers in ways that were contrary to my requests, it was easy for me to wonder and ask "why?" Did I not pray often enough? Maybe I didn't make my request perfectly clear. Did I do something to upset God? If God loves me, why didn't He give me what I asked for?

I have since tried to grow in maturity. I remind myself that God does love me. Maybe that's the reason that He doesn't give us everything that we ask. Just like I know what's better for my children, God knows what's better for me. I see the here and now. I make plans for today, next week, and sometimes next year. God knows the plans for my entire life and my children's lives too.

> *"When I was a child, I talked like a child, I thought like a child, I reasoned like a child. When I became a man, I put the ways of childhood behind me. For now we see only a reflection as in a mirror; then we shall see face to face. Now I know in part; then I shall know fully, even as I am fully known." (1 Corinthians 13:11 - 12)*

According to this passage, I will eventually see God face to face. I'll leave the foolish ways of this world behind and understand God's plan and actions in my life. Then I'll thank Him for giving me the sandwich instead of the ketchup.

DAY 14 – MY BODY IS A TEMPLE

I was using the bathroom one day and Addison flings the door open and runs in. "Can I help you?" I asked sarcastically. She quickly responded, "Yes. I'll have a McDouble-plain and a sweet tea." ...oh boy!

Initially I was annoyed by my two-year-old ruining my privacy in the bathroom, but that soon changed. I went from annoyed to convicted pretty quickly. When hearing the question "Can I help you?" she immediately thought to respond with an order for McDonalds – just like she was going through the drive-thru. Not just any order that she made up on her own; this was an order that she heard frequently from my husband and me. What was I teaching her?

There's nothing wrong with eating fast food – in moderation, but if my daughter had our usual orders memorized by the time she was two and a half, we may be visiting the golden arches more often than we should. That's not what I want to be teaching my children.

The Bible instructs us to take care of our bodies.

> *"Do you not know that your bodies are temples of the Holy Spirit, who is in you, whom you have received from God? You are not your own; you were bought at a price. Therefore honor God with your bodies." (1 Corinthians 6:19-20)*

While this passage of scripture is directly referencing the topic of keeping our bodies sexually pure, I believe that it can apply to other areas as well.

We are told many times in the Bible about the importance of rest. Our bodies were not designed to be constantly busy. Even God took time to rest after he finished creating the world. If God took time to rest, we should too. Rest allows our bodies to function normally. Times of quiet rest also allow us opportunities to focus on listening to God.

If I am honoring God with my body, would I make a habit of stuffing it with fast food and sweet treats all the time? I want my children to know how important it is to eat foods that will help our bodies grow and be healthy. I also want them to understand the importance of getting some exercise. They don't need to run marathons (unless they want to), but I want them to be able to follow the calling that God has on their lives. I want them to be able to go out and do great things for Him. It's harder to muster up the energy to volunteer at a shelter, go on a mission trip, or even perform well in our careers if our bodies are unhealthy and sluggish. After all, if I choose to follow Jesus, my body belongs to Him to be used for His service. Are you treating your body like a temple?

DAY 15 – HUMOR

How long does it take to scrub an entire bottle of red fingernail polish off of a two-year-old's legs?
If you guessed 58 minutes, you would be correct.

I'll admit that while I was feverishly scrubbing my daughter's legs (and the floor) I did not find humor in the situation. I was worried that I wouldn't be able to remove the bright red nail polish from the hardwood floors of our parsonage. I was listening to Addison scream and cry because she didn't want me take off all of her pretty polish. Not to mention that I was doing all of this scrubbing and toddler wrestling while I was pregnant with my second child.

When situations like this arise, I try to ask myself the question, "In the grand scheme of life, will this really be that bad?" Most times the answer is "no." I don't really enjoy cleaning up messes, but most times when I look back on these situations, they end up being funny. As I recall, my Little Addison looked so cute completely covered in red nail polish. My own mother often recalls the story of me smearing a bottle of chocolate syrup all over the house when I was just a toddler.

My daughter loves to tell stories like this to everyone. She gets a kick out of seeing people's reactions and loves to make them laugh. Even at eight years old, Addison understands that humor is powerful and she's not wrong.

> *"A cheerful heart is good medicine,*
> *but a crushed spirit dries up the bones."*
> *(Proverbs 17:22)*

It has been said that laughter is the best medicine. I hope that this story gives you a daily dose today and reminds you to find humor in something every day.

DAY 16 – SPAGHETTI O CONTENTMENT

Addison informed me during lunch today, "Mommy, you make the best Spaghetti O's I ever seen!" I'm glad she was impressed.

Addison loves Spaghetti O's. She was on a kick where she requested them for lunch every day. She ate them for a few months and never got sick of them. She was perfectly content eating the same lunch every single day. I'm glad that she chose something so simple for me to prepare.

Addison's contentment made me think of how much I can complain about wanting something new. It reminded me of the Israelites when they were wandering in the desert. They were grumbling about not having food, so God sent them manna from heaven.

"In the desert the whole community grumbled against Moses and Aaron. The Israelites said to them, 'If only we had died by the Lord's hand in Egypt! There we sat around pots of meat and ate all the food we wanted, but you have brought us out into this desert to starve this entire assembly to death.'

Then the Lord said to Moses, 'I will rain down bread from heaven for you. The people are to go out each day and gather enough for that day. In this way I will test them and see whether they will follow my instructions. On the sixth day they are to prepare what they bring in, and that is to be twice as much as they gather on the other days.'" *(Exodus 16:2-5)*

God heard their grumbling and decided to give them manna. According to Exodus 16, the manna was white like coriander seed and tasted like wafers made with honey. That sounds pretty good to me. He blessed them with this food every single morning (except for the Sabbath).

Were the Israelites content with God's gift? No. Later on they began grumbling again about their shortage of water, so God tells Moses to strike a rock with his staff. Water came out of the rock for all of the people to drink. Were they happy then? Nope. They began to grumble and complain about only having manna to eat.

"The rabble with them began to crave other food, and again the Israelites started wailing and said, 'If only we had meat to eat! We remember the fish we ate in Egypt at no cost—also the cucumbers, melons, leeks, onions and garlic. But now we have lost our appetite; we never see anything but this manna!' (Numbers 11:4-6)

God became angry with the people for grumbling. He sent them quail to eat in the evening. The piles of quail were three feet deep. There was meat for everyone, but God caused the meat to make the grumblers sick and they died because of their complaining.

I pray that I will be content with the manna (or Spaghetti O's) that God has given me and that I will always count my blessings.

CHAPTER 17 – PEAS

We are sitting at the table eating dinner.

Me: Noah, you can't get up from the table until you eat a spoonful of peas.

Noah: *whining* I don't want to. I don't like them.

Me: Everyone else ate some peas. They seemed to like them.

Noah: *still whining* But God made us all different!

Touche

Clearly my son has been paying attention to his recent Sunday School lessons. God did make each of us different. That's what makes our families and circles of friends so interesting. This little example with peas reminded me of the body of Christ.

"Just as a body, though one, has many parts, but all its many parts form one body, so it is with Christ. For we were all baptized by one Spirit so as to form one body—whether Jews or Gentiles, slave or free—and we were all given the one Spirit to drink. Even so the body is not made up of one part but of many.

Now if the foot should say, 'Because I am not a hand, I do not belong to the body,' it would not for that reason stop being part of the body. And if the ear should say, 'Because I am not an eye, I do not belong to the body,' it would not for that reason stop being part of the body. If the whole body were an eye, where would the sense of hearing be? If the whole body were an ear, where would the sense of smell be? But in fact God has placed the parts in the body, every one of them, just as he wanted them to be. If they were all one part, where would the body be? As it is, there are many parts, but one body.

The eye cannot say to the hand, 'I don't need you!' And the head cannot say to the feet, 'I don't need you!' On the contrary, those parts of the body that seem to be weaker are indispensable, and the parts that we think are less honorable we treat with special honor. And the parts that are unpresentable are treated with special modesty, while our presentable parts need no special treatment. But God has put the body together, giving greater honor to the parts that lacked it, so that there should be no division in the body, but that its parts should have equal concern for each other. If one part suffers, every part suffers with it; if one part is honored, every part rejoices with it.

Now you are the body of Christ, and each one of you is a part of it." (1 Corinthians 12:12-27)

We are the body of Christ. Each one of us has a special design and purpose. God has given us different likes, dislikes, and talents. Our physical appearances are different too. He made us each unique and yet designed us to work together.

I can't expect my children to like the same things when they are all very different little people. I decided to let Noah get up from the table without eating his spoonful of peas – just this once.

DAY 18 – GUM

This too has passed.

This Facebook entry may seem a bit vague, but my close family members knew exactly what I was posting about at the time. My youngest child, Owen, found a pack of Trident gum in my purse. He decided to help himself to about six pieces before I found him hiding with a little pile of gum wrappers.

At first, I was concerned. I knew that he would be okay eating a piece of gum, but how many pieces is too many for a two-year-old? I phoned my sister (she's a nurse) to see if a hospital visit was in order. She insisted that gum doesn't stay in your stomach and that it would pass just like anything else that you eat. I decided to just keep an eye on him for the next few days. About three days later… the gum passed. Owen didn't seem to be phased by it at all, but I breathed a huge sigh of relief.

Growing up, my family used to say "this too shall pass" any time something upsetting happened. (It was usually repeated to toddlers multiple times each day when they were voicing their displeasure over something.) It was a reminder that even though something unpleasant was happening, it probably wouldn't last long. Things would get better and we would be happy again.

> *"Sing the praises of the Lord, you his faithful people; praise his holy name.*
> *For his anger lasts only a moment, but his favor lasts a lifetime; weeping may stay for the night, but rejoicing comes in the morning."*
> *(Psalm 30:4-5)*

Weeping may last for the night, but rejoicing comes in the morning. I'm thankful that God does not leave us in our sorrows. He sends people our way to cry with us and help us through our difficult times. The Holy Spirit can bring us comfort and peace. Our hard times will eventually pass. Did you know that the phrase "came to pass" appears in the King James Version of the Bible almost 500 times? Situations "come to pass." Life does not stay the same. If you are going through a time of weeping, don't give up. There will be better times ahead – rejoicing comes in the morning.

DAY 19 – BORN AGAIN

Noah just told me to "PUT OWEN BACK IN YOUR BELLY!" (Owen wrecked one of Noah's Lego creations.) LOL

I tried to explain to Noah that his little brother wouldn't fit back into my belly. He insisted that we should at least try to get him back in there and that he could be born again later. After a few minutes of trying to reason with my five-year-old, I was reminded of a story in the book of John.

"Now there was a Pharisee, a man named Nicodemus who was a member of the Jewish ruling council. He came to Jesus at night and said, 'Rabbi, we know that you are a teacher who has come from God. For no one could perform the signs you are doing if God were not with him.'

Jesus replied, 'Very truly I tell you, no one can see the kingdom of God unless they are born again.'

'How can someone be born when they are old?'
Nicodemus asked. 'Surely they cannot enter a
second time into their mother's womb to be born!'
*   Jesus answered, 'Very truly I tell you, no one*
can enter the kingdom of God unless they are born
of water and the Spirit. Flesh gives birth to flesh,
but the Spirit gives birth to spirit.'" (John 3:1-6)

We are to be born again, but not from our
mother's womb(thank goodness). Jesus tells
Nicodemus that we need to have a spiritual birth in
order to go to heaven.

When we are born physically, we enter a new world
and experience everything for the first time. We see
and hear things differently than we did before. Sure,
we can see and hear in the womb, but our mother's
voice is clearer when we are born. We can also finally
see her face and interact with her on a different level.

A similar thing happens when we are born of the
Spirit. When we choose to make Jesus our Lord and
the Holy Spirit enters us, we are "born again" by the
Spirit. Just as after our physical birth, we see and hear
things differently after our spiritual birth. We hear
God's voice more clearly. We can see everyone
around us in a different light. We become more aware
of our Father's ways. I am looking forward to the day
when I enter heaven and I can see His face more
clearly too.

DAY 20 – CORRECTION

Addison was looking out our kitchen window one morning.
Addison: *excitedly* Mama! Mama! Penwin!
Me: No Addy, that's not a penguin – it's a robin.
Addison: *cheerfully* Oh, okay!

I remember that morning very well. It was still pretty cool outside, but Spring was not too far off. Addison was jumping up and down excitedly and pointing at the birds outside. She had just turned two years old and was still amazed at everything in the world around her. She was so happy to spot some "penwins" in the yard!

I hesitated a moment before correcting her. I didn't want to crush her feelings of excitement, but I also didn't want her to think that robins were actually penguins. I wanted her to be correct and to know the truth.

To my surprise, Addison didn't have any hurt feelings. She accepted my correction immediately. She was even happy about it.

The Bible mentions instruction, correction, and discipline many times, especially in the book of Proverbs.

> *"A fool spurns a parent's discipline,*
> *but whoever heeds correction shows prudence."*
> *(Proverbs 15:5)*

I know that I don't always accept correction with a happy heart. Sometimes pride steps in and makes me argue my point. When the Holy Spirit convicts me, I try to rationalize my thoughts and actions to God instead of just accepting His correction. I hope that I will learn to heed correction as easily and as happily as my daughter did on that day. I know that God loves me even more than I love my daughter, and that He wants me to know and follow the truth as well.

DAY 21 – LIPSTICK GUILT

Addison peeks around the corner and gives me some "guilty eyes." I ask what she is up to because she "has guilt all over her face." She whispered, "It's not guilt, Mommy, - it's your lipstick."

It was quiet that evening. Before I had children, quiet = peaceful. After becoming a mom however, quiet = suspicion. I called for Addison to see what she was doing. Instead of running into the room and jumping on my lap, she hid from me and only peeked some "guilty eyes" around the corner. I immediately knew that she had to be up to no good.

She managed to open the bathroom door and get into my makeup bag. She had light pink lipstick all over her lips. I'm still not sure if she was trying to look like a pretty princess or apply for a position with the clowns at the circus.

Did she really think that I wouldn't notice? It was pretty obvious. She didn't understand the word "guilt" at the time, but she sure felt it. She reminded me of how we sometimes act toward God when we know that we've done something wrong. Adam and Eve were the first example of guilt. Unfortunately, we still follow their example at times today.

"When the woman saw that the fruit of the tree was good for food and pleasing to the eye, and also desirable for gaining wisdom, she took some and ate it. She also gave some to her husband, who was with her, and he ate it.

Then the eyes of both of them were opened, and they realized they were naked; so they sewed fig leaves together and made coverings for themselves.

Then the man and his wife heard the sound of the Lord God as he was walking in the garden in the cool of the day, and they hid from the Lord God among the trees of the garden. But the Lord God called to the man, 'Where are you?'

He answered, 'I heard you in the garden, and I was afraid because I was naked; so I hid.'

And he said, 'Who told you that you were naked? Have you eaten from the tree that I commanded you not to eat from?'

The man said, 'The woman you put here with me—she gave me some fruit from the tree, and I ate it.'

Then the Lord God said to the woman, 'What is this you have done?'

The woman said, 'The serpent deceived me, and I ate.'" (Genesis 3:6-13)

My daughter didn't even know the story about Adam & Eve and yet, here she was, following in their footsteps. Will we ever learn? We cannot disobey and then hide from God. It's best to just admit when we've messed up. If we ask, He'll forgive us. He'll wipe the "lipstick" away and give us a fresh start.

DAY 22 – HEAVENLY COOKIES

Noah's question of the day: "Mommy, are there cookies in Heaven?" (He asked with an Oreo in each hand.) I told him that there probably are cookies in Heaven. He replied, "Good! I was just checking."

If I told Noah that there were no cookies in Heaven, he may have changed his mind about wanting to go there. The boy loves his cookies. Now, I don't know for certain if there are actually cookies in Heaven, but I don't know that there aren't cookies either. What I do know is that the Bible says that one day God will spread a wonderful feast for everyone. Desserts are included in a feast right?

"On this mountain the Lord Almighty will prepare
a feast of rich food for all peoples,
a banquet of aged wine—
the best of meats and the finest of wines.
On this mountain he will destroy
the shroud that enfolds all peoples,
the sheet that covers all nations;
he will swallow up death forever.
The Sovereign Lord will wipe away the tears
from all faces;
he will remove his people's disgrace
from all the earth.
The Lord has spoken.
In that day they will say,

'Surely this is our God;
we trusted in him, and he saved us.
This is the Lord, we trusted in him;
let us rejoice and be glad in his salvation.'"
(Isaiah 25:6-9)

I'm looking forward to that day. There will be no more tears and no more death. We'll have no worries or cares. Everything that brings us sadness in this world will be taken away. On that day we will rejoice in our salvation and have a great feast with our Awesome God. And just maybe, eat some cookies.

DAY 23 - NINJAS

I was explaining to Noah what a "veteran" is and about the different branches of our military. He enthusiastically responds, "I want to fight for our country! – But I wanna be a ninja – What part has the ninjas?" So does anyone know what branch of the military ninjas fall under? My four-year-old is really wanting to know.

Part of me was so proud that my son wanted to grow up to serve his country. I could just imagine him standing tall in a nice, crisp uniform. Another part of me was not so fond of hearing those words come out of my son. If he joins the military, I may have to watch him go away to fight in a foreign land. He could be killed or I may never see him again.

This conversation reminded me to pray for all of the brave men and women who are currently serving our country in the military. They face challenges and situations that I know nothing about. I can't even imagine what they sometimes endure. They not only face the threat of battle, but they miss out on many things that we take for granted everyday like going shopping or attending a sporting event. They even miss important moments like birthday parties and weddings. I am so grateful for their sacrifice.

I not only think of the soldiers, but their friends and families as well. I think of their children who grow up seeing their deployed parent for only a few weeks at a time. I often pray especially for mothers of soldiers. I imagine that it would be very difficult not being able to communicate with a son or daughter, knowing that they are in harm's way. I pray that they would have peace and hope.

If my son does grow up to become a soldier, I hope that I will remember to put my trust in God and know that He is in control. He has a plan and purpose for my son's life. Until then, I am happy with Noah being a little ninja.

DAY 24 – BAPTISM

    I was watching a clip of our church's latest baptism service on my computer this morning.
Noah: Are they vaporizing people?
Me: You mean BAPTISING people?
Noah: Oh yeah…that.
LOL

    Noah's comment gave me a morning chuckle, but also an opportunity to talk to him about baptism. He had questions about what baptizing means and why people want to do it. I tried my best to explain in terms that a four-year-old would understand.

    I told Noah that when someone gets baptized, it's a symbol of them changing their life. When someone loves Jesus and wants to follow him, they usually get baptized. All of the bad stuff they used to do is washed away when they are dunked under the water and their "old self" is dead. Then they rise up out of the water like Jesus rose from the dead and they have a new fresh life.

Noah seemed to grasp this concept, but still asked why we do baptisms. I told him that we get baptized to be obedient to Jesus. Jesus told us to tell other people about him and to baptize them.

> *"Then Jesus came to them and said, 'All authority in heaven and on earth has been given to me. Therefore go and make disciples of all nations, baptizing them in the name of the Father and of the Son and of the Holy Spirit, and teaching them to obey everything I have commanded you. And surely I am with you always, to the very end of the age.'" (Matthew 28:18-20)*

Later on that evening, I was giving Noah a bath. I stepped across the hallway to get him some pajamas while he was finishing his bath. Addison was helping me keep an eye on him in the tub. After a moment, I heard giggling. I peeked my head into the bathroom to see Addison dunking Noah under the water saying "in the name of the Father, the Son, and the Holy Spirit." He wanted to practice getting baptized.

DAY 25 - WITCHES

Our family was getting groceries at a little country store near our home. My husband was pushing Noah is the shopping cart. I was following behind holding Addison's hand.

Suddenly Noah leaned close to my husband and whispered, "Go faster, Daddy." My husband didn't really pay much attention to him. He just assumed that he didn't want to be stuck in the cart and wanted to get our shopping over with as soon as possible.

After a few minutes, Noah again whispered to my husband, "Go faster, Daddy. The witches are coming." My husband chalked this comment up to a wild three-year-old imagination and we all continued on with our shopping.

After several more minutes, Noah appeared to be genuinely frightened and said to us, "We have to go faster. Witches are coming." I tried to calm him down and assure him that there wouldn't be any witches in the grocery store.

I racked my brain trying to think of where he would come up with such an idea. I didn't read any books about witches that day and I didn't recall seeing any in his cartoons either. We continued putting groceries in our cart.

49

When we moved to an open area of the grocery store, Noah suddenly threw his arm out and wildly pointed. He started yelling, "THERE ARE THE WITCHES! AND THEY HAVE A WITCH BABY!"

Everyone in the grocery store was looking at him. I followed his little pointed finger across the way - two Amish women wearing black dresses and black bonnets were getting groceries. And they had a baby with a black bonnet riding in their cart.

I was mortified! I put my hand over Noah's mouth to stop his repeated yelling. I explained to him very loudly that the women weren't witches – they were Amish.

> *"A wise son brings joy to his father,*
> *but a foolish son brings grief to his mother."*
> *(Proverbs 10:1)*

Looking back on this story now is very amusing, but at that time, this mama was horribly embarrassed. I wanted to hide behind anything available. I also felt bad for the Amish women who were obviously not amused by my son's enthusiastic accusations.

I wonder if this is how God feels when I make a foolish judgement about someone. This little example reminds me to try to hold my tongue. To not judge someone until I actually know them. I want my words and actions to bring joy to my Father.

DAY 26 – GOOD CHOICES

I was driving the kids home this evening on winding country roads when we saw a deer running down through a field. It was headed straight for us. Addison yells out of her window toward the deer, "MAKE GOOD CHOICES! MAKE GOOD CHOICES!" I slowed the vehicle. The deer came to a halt at the edge of the road and then quickly turned around to run back the way it came.

Thank goodness the deer decided to listen to my daughter! We avoided a collision thanks to the deer's wise decision. It was comical listening to my daughter call out to the deer, but it also made me stop and think. Wouldn't it be nice to have someone yell that same thing to me every time that I had an important decision to make? "MAKE GOOD CHOICES! MAKE GOOD CHOICES!" It would be a great reminder to choose my actions wisely.

Jesus tells us in the book of Matthew about the importance of following his commands and making wise decisions.

> *"Therefore everyone who hears these words of mine and puts them into practice is like a wise man who built his house on the rock. The rain came down, the streams rose, and the winds blew and beat against that house; yet it did not fall, because it had its foundation on the rock. But everyone who hears these words of mine and does not put them into practice is like a foolish man who built his house on sand. The rain came down, the streams rose, and the winds blew and beat against that house, and it fell with a great crash."*
> *(Matthew 7:24-27)*

When the storms of life come, I don't want my house to fall with a great crash! While I don't have someone to yell in my face, I do have a reminder from Jesus to be wise. I need to practice his teachings. I need to base my decisions on His word and ask Him to help me make good choices. That way my house will not fall and I won't become road kill on the highway of life.

DAY 27 – RULES

"Don't lick the doorstop!" - a phrase that I never thought that I would say, until I became a parent.

"Why are there pieces of Christmas tree in your diaper? Don't put pieces of Christmas tree in your diaper!" - another one of those things I never expected to say.

I know that as a parent, it's important to teach my children what they should and should not do. I just never expected that I would have to come up with seemingly obvious rules – "Don't eat that. Don't punch your brother/sister. Don't store things in your diaper/underwear."

I wonder if that's how God felt when He was giving all of the instructions of the law in the Old Testament. The book of Leviticus is full of rules that would seem obvious to many people: "Do not steal. Do not eat this or that. Do not make your daughter become a prostitute. Do not lie. Do not offer your children as sacrifices to Molek." The list goes on and on and on. God had to be shaking his head and feeling disgusted with his people, especially when they broke these rules.

I'm so thankful that God sent Jesus to become our ultimate sacrifice. Not only did Jesus save us and take away the need for us to sacrifice, but he made the list of commands much shorter and easier to understand.

> *"Hearing that Jesus had silenced the Sadducees, the Pharisees got together. One of them, an expert in the law, tested him with this question: 'Teacher, which is the greatest commandment in the Law?'*
>
> *Jesus replied: "'Love the Lord your God with all your heart and with all your soul and with all your mind.' This is the first and greatest commandment. And the second is like it: 'Love your neighbor as yourself.' All the Law and the Prophets hang on these two commandments."* (Matthew 22:34-40)

Love God and love your neighbor. Thank you Jesus for simplifying our rules.

DAY 28 – ADMIRER

The phone rings. Doug, my husband, answers it and says to me, "It's Donald Trump and he wants to talk to you."

Noah immediately says, "He must have a crush on Mommy. He calls here to talk to her all the time!" LOL

We were nearing the end of the presidential election season for 2016. My husband and I received countless calls every day from people wanting our votes. That call was no different from the others. Just a recording of Donald Trump asking for my vote.

It was interesting that my kindergartener could make the connection that spending time talking with someone = having a crush on them. He asked me if I was going to marry Donald. I explained to Noah that I was already happily married and would not be dating Mr. Trump.

My children notice who I spend my time talking to. If they notice a few more phone calls from a certain individual, they will surely also notice who I talk with in person at home, church, school, etc. I want my kids to see me spending lots of time with their father so that there is no doubt that we love each other.

I also want my children to see me spending time with my Heavenly Father. I want to spend so much time praying and reading scripture that my kids will know that I love God and want to pursue Him with all of my heart. I want them to know that my relationship with God is extremely important.

When Jesus was on earth, he spent much of his time talking with his Father.

> *"Each day Jesus was teaching at the temple, and each evening he went out to spend the night on the hill called the Mount of Olives, and all the people came early in the morning to hear him at the temple." (Luke 21:37,38)*

Jesus's evenings on the Mount of Olives were spent in prayer. I imagine that this is where he found some rest and was able to recharge for his long days of teaching.

My goal is to model Jesus's behavior. To spend every night talking to God before I sleep. Then maybe my children will notice and realize who I truly admire.

DAY 29 – FOOLS

Noah: Mama, what's for dinner?
Me: Chicken Florentine
Noah: Aww! I don't LIKE pancakes!

Apparently my son had a very mixed-up view of Chicken Florentine. I don't think that he had even tasted the dish before that evening, but he was very adamant that he didn't like it and wasn't going to eat any pancakes. I tried to explain to him that the dish was made up of chicken, garlic, cream, & spinach and that pancakes were definitely not an ingredient. He continued to argue with me until we both became frustrated.

The Bible speaks many times about foolish people spouting off their opinions. I was reminded of this verse:

> *"Fools find no pleasure in understanding, but delight in airing their own opinions."*
> *(Proverbs 18:2)*

My son certainly had his own opinion and was not afraid to air it. This is understandable coming from a preschooler, but I've learned that fools can also be much older. They can be found in every stage of life. In fact, if you have ever spent any amount of time on social media, you have probably come across some fools delighting in airing their opinions.

It can be very tempting to argue with foolish people. I find myself wanting to show them another fact or point of view. If you have ever tried this, you know that it's almost always unfruitful. Some of the simplest comments can turn into discouraging, hate-filled conversations within moments. We are told about this in the book of 2 Timothy.

> *"Don't have anything to do with foolish and stupid arguments, because you know they produce quarrels. And the Lord's servant must not be quarrelsome but must be kind to everyone, able to teach, not resentful. Opponents must be gently instructed, in the hope that God will grant them repentance leading them to a knowledge of the truth, and that they will come to their senses and escape from the trap of the devil, who has taken them captive to do his will."*
> *(2 Timothy 2:23-26)*

This is wonderful advice. When I come across a fool who is trying to stir up trouble. I am to give a simple instruction or example and then leave it to God to show them the truth. My arguing with them will probably only make things worse. I'll try to remember this advice, and in the meantime, try not to be a fool myself.

DAY 30 – GOD IN EVERYTHING

How do I relate my daily conversations and activities back to God?

Some people are surprised that I can relate almost everything that happens to me back to God. I tell them that God is everywhere and in everything if they take the time to seek Him. The book of Romans tells us that God can be seen clearly.

> *"For since the creation of the world God's invisible qualities—his eternal power and divine nature—have been clearly seen, being understood from what has been made, so that people are without excuse." (Romans 1: 20)*

How can I look outside and see beautiful landscapes and think that it happened by accident? I can't. And if I can't do that, how can I look at my friends & family and think that they were created without design or purpose? I can't.

I have been extremely blessed. It is my hope that reading this devotional has helped you to see God in all of the little things around you every day and that you will grow closer to Him.

A Towel Filled With Toothpaste

ABOUT THE AUTHOR

Kimberly Henry has a BSW from Lock Haven University of Pennsylvania. She currently works part-time as a church secretary and childrens church leader. She has been married to her husband, Pastor Doug Henry, since 2003. They have a daughter, Addison, and two sons, Noah & Owen. Kimberly sings and plays drums in a band and has been a member of her local MOPS (Mothers of Preschoolers) group since its beginning seven years ago.

41961269R00042

Made in the USA
Middletown, DE
27 March 2017